W9-BCX-135

Created

to

Dream

Created
to
Dream

**The 6 Phases God Uses
to Grow Your Faith**

RICK WARREN

ZONDERVAN
BOOKS

ZONDERVAN BOOKS

Created to Dream
Copyright © 2023 by Rick Warren

Requests for information should be addressed to:
Zondervan, 3900 *Sparks Dr. SE,* Grand Rapids, Michigan 49546

Zondervan titles may be purchased in bulk for educational, business, fundraising, or sales promotional use. For information, please email SpecialMarkets@Zondervan.com.

ISBN 978-0-310-36784-0 (hardcover)
ISBN 978-0-310-36786-4 (audio)
ISBN 978-0-310-36785-7 (ebook)

Cover design: Ashe Correa, Azrielle Tamez, Faith King
Cover illustrations: pikisuperstar / Freepik
Interior design: Kait Lamphere
Editorial: Amanda Halash, Abby Watson, Kim Tanner, Allison Dolbeer
General editors: Buddy Owens and Molly Parker

Printed in the United States of America

23 24 25 26 27 LBC 5 4 3 2 1

Contents

CHAPTER 1

How Faith and Dreaming Are *Connected*

"I know the plans I have for you," declares the Lord, "plans to prosper you and not to harm you, plans to give you hope and a future."

Jeremiah 29:11 (NIV)

You were created to dream.

Dreaming has an essential role in developing your faith and helping you become the kind of person God has always intended you to be. There is an important connection between dreaming and believing, between your imagination and your growth. Without a dream, you get stuck. But with God-inspired dreams, you have almost limitless possibilities.

Before you took your first breath, God had already placed the gift of imagination into your brain. God hardwired creativity into every cell of your body. The Bible says you were created in God's image.[1] Part of what is included in being made in God's image is the ability to dream and create something out of nothing.

This ability to dream of something you have not yet experienced is a God-given capacity that sets humans apart

A great dream is a statement of faith.

3

from the rest of God's creation. Fish can't imagine flying or even living out of water. Birds can't imagine living underwater. But humans have dreamed of both of these, and so much more, for ages.

Dreaming is an important part of what makes you human. People dream great dreams. They imagine creating and doing things often years before those things become reality. Everything that humanity has accomplished in history started as a dream. Napoleon once said, "Imagination rules the world!"

Your dreams profoundly shape your identity, your happiness, your achievements, and your fulfillment. But God-inspired dreaming is far more important than just these benefits. Dreaming has *eternal* implications too. Dreaming is always the first step God uses in his process to change your life for the better. Everything starts as a dream.

God dreams. Just look around! Everything in the universe is something God dreamed up. You can't get past the first phrase of the first verse of the first chapter of the Bible without coming face-to-face with God's creativity. Genesis 1:1 says, *"In the beginning God created."*[2] God imagined and spoke everything into existence. It all began in the mind of God. The Bible says, *"All things were made by him, and nothing was made without him. In him there was life, and that life was the light of all people.*"[3]

Just by looking at nature, we can learn a lot about God. We can see that God is powerful. We can see that God loves beauty. We can see that God cares about details. We can see that God is organized. He has created all kinds of coordinated systems that interrelate—in the galaxies, in our environment, in our bodies, and in many other ways. Science continues to uncover new relationships between systems that we were previously unaware of.

Most of all, we see God's *creativity* in nature. Our Creator is extravagantly creative. Just think of all the plants and animals that fill our planet. He dreamed up the millions of variations in creatures and vegetation—and then he created you. He gave you the ability to create too, by giving you the capacity to dream, imagine, and plan.

Children are naturally creative dreamers. We learn by playing make-believe. You dreamed of doing things in your mind long before you actually did them. Yes, children are instinctively creative dreamers who imagine all kinds of things that adults know are "impossible." What happens to all that joyful creativity and dreaming? It gets crushed, stuffed, suppressed, stifled, and destroyed by others over time. It's tragic but true. Typically, the older we get, the less we imagine and create.

What does all of this have to do with your spiritual development? Everything! That's what this book is about. As I mentioned, most people are unaware of the important connection between dreaming and faith. But men and women of deep faith have always been great dreamers. They didn't stop dreaming after childhood. The Bible is filled with examples of adult dreamers: Abraham, Joseph, Moses, Ruth, Esther, and many more. Instead of settling for the way things are in the world, people with strong faith imagine the possibilities of what could happen if they just trusted God a little bit more.

Great faith inspires great dreams.
Great dreams require great faith.

In many ways, a great dream is a statement of faith. Certainly, announcing your dream publicly requires faith because other people are likely to reject it. To courageously imagine or dream of a better future for yourself, for your family, or for others is an act of faith. You are saying, "I believe that things *can* change and can be different, and I believe that God will enable me to accomplish it!" Trusting God always makes God happy. The Bible says, *"Without faith it is impossible to please God, because anyone who comes to him must believe that he exists and that he rewards those who earnestly seek him."*[4] I believe God is pleased that you are reading this right now. You matter to God, and he is not finished with your life. This is the beginning of something wonderful.

> While you're working on your dream, God will be working on your character.

In this short book, I'll summarize the six phases of the process God uses to grow our faith and develop our character. This process is illustrated over and over in the lives of people in the Bible. More important, this faith-building process will be repeated over and over in *your* life as God keeps moving you toward spiritual and emotional maturity.

The growth process begins with dreaming, but dreaming is just the first phase. There are five more phases, and if you don't understand the many ways that your dream (and your faith) will be tested, you'll be tempted to give up. But dreaming is the step that gets the ball rolling. It is a catalyst for personal change. And *that* is what God is most concerned about: preparing you for life with him in eternity.

Here's a little secret: while you are more

interested in reaching your dream on earth, God is more interested in building your character for heaven. Why? Because God has long-range plans for you that will far outlast your brief time on earth. God has a longer view of you. He's looking at your life in light of eternity. The fact is this: *any* goal or dream that you envision happening here on earth will be short-term because everything on earth is temporary. We're just passing through. This is just the warm-up act before the real show takes place on the other side of death. Life on earth doesn't last. But life in eternity will last forever.

When you die, you're not going to take your career to heaven. You're not going to take your clothes or your cars or your cash either. You'll leave everything behind. The only thing you'll take into eternity is you! That means your character and the person you chose to become. The Bible is blunt: *"We brought nothing into the world, and we can take nothing out of it."*[5] That's why God considers *what you become* on earth far more important than *what you do* while you're here. So while you're working on your dream, God will be working on your character.

Here's the good news: God promises that if you cooperate with him, he will complete the makeover in your heart. The Bible says, *"I am certain that God, who began the good work within you, will continue his work until it is finally finished on the day when Christ Jesus returns."*[6]

So here's the first choice you need to make: Will you choose God's dream for your life, or will you choose your own dream? Or will you let someone else impose their dream on you? Let me be clear: God has *not* promised to bless everything you dream up! Why? Because not all of your dreams, goals, passions, and ambitions are what's best for you. Some dreams are unhelpful. Some are harmful. Some dreams end up being nightmares, and some lead to disaster. The Bible says, *"Some people think they are doing right, but in the end it leads to death."*[7] This is why you should want God's dream for your life, rather than your own. God's dream for your life is infinitely better than any dream you could come up with on your own. It won't be easy, and it won't be quick. This book will explain that. But it will be worth it.

God's dream for you is not an afterthought. He already knew what he wanted you to do before he formed you in your mother's womb, and he created you specifically for that purpose. The Bible says, *"We are*

> **Figuring out and following God's dream is a walk of faith.**

God's handiwork, created in Christ Jesus to do good works, which God prepared in advance for us to do."[8]

In Jeremiah 29:11, God made this promise: *"I know the plans I have for you . . . plans to prosper you and not to harm you, plans to give you hope and a future."*[9] God has a plan for your life. You wouldn't be alive if he didn't have a purpose for you. The Bible says in Colossians 1:16, *"Everything, absolutely everything . . . got started in him and finds its purpose in him."*[10] That includes you! God doesn't make mistakes. He never does anything accidentally. He has no second thoughts. He created you for a purpose, and he has a dream for your life.

Following God's dream is infinitely more rewarding than attaining anything you could dream on your own. That's because God's dream for your life has eternal implications. He doesn't want you to live for just the here and now. He wants you to live with eternity in mind. Your time on earth will last only eighty to one hundred years or so, but your time in heaven will last for eternity—and so will God's plan for you.

"God can do anything, you know—far more than you could ever imagine or guess or request in your wildest dreams!"[11]

I don't know about you, but I can dream pretty big dreams. But God's dream exceeds anything I could imagine. And I can tell you this: pursuing God's dream is the greatest adventure you will ever experience.

Consider these benefits of pursuing God's dream for your life: it strengthens your faith, deepens your courage, and builds your character; it stretches your imagination, expands your horizon, and broadens your perspective; it clarifies your priorities, sharpens your thinking, and focuses your energy; and it always—*always*—reveals something new of the wonder and glory of God. Nothing else in life will do what God's dream will do for you. You will find no greater fulfillment than when you're doing what God created you to do.

Stepping into God's Dream

There are many things in life that you have no control over. You didn't choose your parents. You didn't choose when or where you were born. You didn't choose your race or your gender. But there is one choice you have complete control over, and that is whether you will accept God's invitation to pursue his dream for your life.

So how do you figure out what God's dream is? And more than that, how do you follow it? Figuring out and following God's dream is a walk of faith. His dream usually is not spelled out in complete detail. You discover it one step at a time. The Bible says, *"The way of the righteous is like the first gleam of dawn, which shines ever brighter until the full light of day."*[12] That means God's dream dawns on you. It becomes more and more clear with every step you take.

The pursuit of God's dream requires a lot of patience. Patience is one of the most common tools God uses to build your faith. In fact, it takes more faith to wait than to take a risk, because waiting forces you to decide: Will you continue to trust God, or will you give up and walk away?

Isaiah 7:9 says, *"If you do not stand firm in your faith, you will not stand at all."*[13] So how is your faith? Is it strong or weak? Is it steady or stretched? These are important questions to answer because Jesus said, *"Everything is possible for the person who has faith."*[14] Jesus also said, *"According to your faith let it be done to you."*[15] In other words, there's a lot riding on your faith! Your faith affects how much God blesses your life.

You might think your faith isn't strong enough

to follow God's dream. Sure it is! The faith you have is enough to get started. Jesus said you need faith only the size of a mustard seed to move a mountain. Do you only have baby faith? Then take a baby step. When you do, your faith will grow for the next step.

Faith is like a muscle. It needs to be exercised and developed. God uses a predictable pattern and process to build your faith. It's what I call the six phases of faith. Once you understand these six phases, you can better cooperate with God in the strengthening of your faith and building of your character while experiencing the great adventure of pursuing God's dream for your life.

The Six Phases of Faith

As a pastor, I'm most often asked this question: "Why is this happening to me? I don't understand it. I thought I was pursuing God's dream, but now I'm ready to give up." Sound familiar? You see, when you don't understand the six phases of faith, you may become resentful, even depressed. You will certainly worry. You may become fearful about the future. And, worst of all, you won't be able to cooperate with what God wants to do in your life. But when you understand the six phases that God takes every believer through—and he takes us through them over and over—then you can say, "Oh, I see, I'm in stage four right now," or stage six or stage two. You will understand what's going on, and you'll be less likely to get discouraged when times are tough.

So let me introduce you to the six phases of faith and their role in pursuing God's dream. Then we will go deeper into each phase in the coming chapters.

Phase 1: Dream

How does God build your faith? He always starts with a dream. Nothing happens until you start dreaming. You have to get an idea, a vision, a goal, or a target. When God wants to work in your life, he gives you a dream about what he wants you to do and the impact he wants you to have in the world. In the next chapter, I will teach you how to figure out God's dream for your life.

Phase 2: Decision

You have to make the decision to go for it! Nothing will happen to your dream until you wake up and put it into action. For every ten dreamers in the world, there is only one decision maker. The only way to move forward in faith is to decide to take a risk. In chapter 3, I will explain six biblical principles for making wise decisions.

Phase 3: Delays

When you pursue your dream, there is always a waiting period. Why does God make you wait? Because God wants to work on *you* before he works on your project. The purpose of the delay phase is to teach you to trust God and to be patient with his timing. How you handle God's waiting rooms of life is a clear measure of the strength of your faith. In chapter 4, I will show you how to keep going when your dream is delayed.

Phase 4: Difficulties

Not only will you have to wait, but you will also have problems while you're waiting. There are problems even when your dream lines up with God's dream, because God is working on your faith and character. In chapter 5, I will share the dos and don'ts of dealing with difficulty.

Finally, the difficulties become so bad that you come to your limit. You've tried everything, you've exhausted all your options ... and now you've reached the fifth phase of faith.

Phase 5: Dead Ends

In the dead-end phase, the situation deteriorates from difficult to impossible. If you are at this stage, congratulations! You are in good company. Even the apostle Paul experienced dead ends. He wrote, *"At that time we were completely overwhelmed, the burden was more than we could bear, in fact we told ourselves that this was the end. Yet we believe now that we had this experience of coming to the end of our tether that we might learn to trust, not in ourselves, but in God who can raise the dead."*[16] God not only can raise people from the dead physically but also can raise people from the dead emotionally. He can raise a dead marriage. He can resurrect a dead career. He can breathe new life where all hope has died. In chapter 6, I will show you how to hold on to your faith when you reach a dead end.

Phase 6: Deliverance

In the end, God delivers. He performs a miracle. He provides a solution. God loves to turn crucifixions into resurrections, hopelessness into victory, and dead ends into deliverance. Why? Because he gets the glory. In chapter 7, I will show you the key to deliverance.

What Phase Are You in Today?

Has God given you a dream? That's what phase one is about. If you don't have a dream, then you're not really living—you're just existing.

Maybe you are in phase two. You have a dream from God but have not made the decision to pursue it. You're still sitting on the fence. You think you're waiting on God, but God is waiting on you. God's word for you in the decision phase is, "Go for it!" Heaven is cheering you on!

You might be in phase three right now. You have a dream and have made the decision, but now it's been delayed. You're asking God, "Why hasn't my prayer been answered yet?" If you're in phase three, remember, you're in God's waiting room. Don't detour, and don't get ahead of God either. Wait for him to open the right door.

Perhaps you are in phase four—you are being tested. What difficulties are you facing while you wait for the dream to be fulfilled? God says, "I know exactly what you're going through. I see it. I'm watching. Don't think I've forgotten you, because I haven't."

Or maybe you are in phase five and are thinking, "I've hit the wall. I'm at a dead end. I'm ready to give up." Well, you're right where God wants you. God is saying to you, "Hang on! Keep on believing! Don't give up!" You're on the verge of phase six: deliverance.

Do you expect God to deliver you? God is faithful. What he promises to do, he will do. Where God guides, he provides. But it doesn't happen overnight.

Where God guides, he provides.

You go through the phases of the dream, the decision, the delays, the difficulties, and the dead ends . . . and then comes the deliverance.

Look again at this verse: *"God can do anything, you know—far more than you could ever imagine or guess or request in your wildest dreams!"*[17] It's as if God says to you, "Think of the greatest dream for your life—I can top it." That's the kind of dream God has for you. It's bigger and better than any ambition, goal, or desire you could ever dream up on your own.

Are you ready to do what God created you to do? God's dream awaits you.

CHAPTER 2

Discovering God's
Dream for You

God can do anything, you know—far more than
you could ever imagine or guess or request
in your wildest dreams! He does it not by
pushing us around but by working within us,
his Spirit deeply and gently within us.

Ephesians 3:20–21 (MSG)

Without a dream, you're not really living—you're just existing.

God's dream determines your destiny and defines your dignity. It's the reason you exist. It's your purpose for living. Without a dream, your life lacks meaning and direction. Without a dream, you will always struggle with your identity—who you are.

There is nothing more important, after you come to know Jesus Christ, than figuring out God's dream for your life. It's only when you discover why God made you and what he wants you to do that life makes sense.

There are many examples of this in the Bible:

- God gave Noah the dream of saving the world from the flood.
- God gave Abraham the dream of being the father of a great nation.
- God gave Joseph the dream of being a leader who would save his people.

- God gave David the dream of building the temple.
- God gave Nehemiah the dream of rebuilding the wall around Jerusalem.
- God gave Paul the dream of going to Rome.

Nothing happens until you start dreaming.

The truth is, everything starts with a dream. Anything that has been created started with somebody dreaming it first. God dreamed up every tree, every mountain, every planet—the whole universe! He dreamed of you too, and then he created you and gave you the ability to be a dreamer. While you can dream up some amazing things, God's dream is custom-made for you. He gives you the ability to dream of new hobbies, new businesses, and new ministries, to dream about making a difference and changing your community, to dream of impacting the world. It all starts with a dream.

Did you realize there are three types of dreams? A dream can be the thoughts and images you have while sleeping. Not all those dreams are good; some are nightmares. Dreams can also be the passions and ambitions you have while awake, and they are more important than the dreams you have while sleeping.

But the third type of dream, God's dream for your life, is the most important dream of all.

How do you know whether a dream is from God or whether you're making it up yourself? How do you know if it's God speaking or if it's the big meal you had last night? When I was a kid, I dreamed of being a rock star so I could play the guitar. But that was *my* dream for me, not God's dream for me. God had a more important dream, one that went beyond anything I could ask for or think up on my own.

One way to know if a dream is from God is to determine whether the dream requires faith. God's dream will always require faith. It will be so big that you can't do it on your own. If you could do it on your own, you wouldn't need faith; and *"without faith it is impossible to please God."*[1]

The second way to know if a dream is from God is to determine whether it aligns with God's Word. God's dream will never contradict God's Word. God will not give you a dream of leaving your family to become a Hollywood star. He won't give you a dream of cheating in business so you can donate the proceeds to your church's building program. Again, God's dream will never contradict God's Word.

> God's dream will never contradict God's Word.

A Custom-Made Dream

God has a *"good, pleasing and perfect will"*[2] for your life. It's not a one-size-fits-all plan. God's dream for you is personal. It's custom-made for the way he shaped you.

There are five important factors that make you *you*. To help you remember them, I created a simple acrostic: SHAPE.

- **S**piritual gifts
- **H**eart
- **A**bilities
- **P**ersonality
- **E**xperiences

You are the only person in the world with your unique, God-given SHAPE. That means you are the only person who can fulfill God's dream for your life. Not only is God's dream personal, it is also positive. It's a plan *"to prosper you and not to harm you . . . to give you hope and a future."*[3]

How do you figure out what God's dream is? Let's look at five steps based on the five letters of the word *dream*.

DEDICATE ALL YOUR LIFE TO GOD

If you want God to show you his dream for your life, then you must be willing to do whatever God wants you to do, even before he tells you to do it. Don't say, "God, show me what you want me to do, and then I'll say yes." Just say yes, and then he will show you what to do.

Romans 12:1 says, *"Offer yourselves as a living sacrifice to God, dedicated to his service."*[4] To discover God's will, the Bible says you must "offer" yourself to God. That means you must dedicate every part of your life—your time, your talents, your treasures, your relationships, your past, your present, and your future—to God's purposes. Sacrifice your agenda for his. Release control of your life to him.

The Bible goes on to say, *"Do not conform yourselves to the standards of this world, but let God transform you inwardly by a complete change of your mind. Then you will be able to know the will of God—what is good and is pleasing to him and is perfect."*[5]

To conform means to fit something into a mold. To transform means to change something from the inside out—and there is a huge difference between the two. God wants to transform you by changing the way you think about him, yourself, life, and the world around you. The number one reason people miss God's dream is because they are trying to fit in with the rest of the world. They become a carbon copy of somebody else instead of being the person God made them to be.

If you want to get serious about figuring out God's dream for your life, then you have to decide if you're going to conform or be transformed. Are you going to settle for the "good life" or God's life, the world's standards or God's standards?

Hebrews 12:1 says, *"Let us strip off anything that slows us down or holds us back . . . and let us run with patience the particular race that God has set before us."*[6] God has a particular life course for you to run. If you are always looking at other people, you'll end up trying to run their race, and there's no way you can win that one. To know God's will, you have to stop conforming to the world's standards and let God transform you into the person he designed you to be.

What is God's will like? It's good, pleasing, and perfect (Romans 12:2). The Greek word translated "perfect" means God's will fits you—you're just what you want to be, ought to be, could be, and should be. In other words, you're exactly what you were created to be.

So the first thing you must do to discover God's

dream for your life is to dedicate all your life to God. The apostle Paul says in Acts 20:24, *"My life is worth nothing to me unless I use it for finishing the work assigned me by the Lord Jesus."*[7]

Have you done that? Have you dedicated your life to him? Pursuing God's dream for your life is a walk of faith, and the very first step is placing your faith in Jesus Christ to forgive your sins. That's the starting point. Jesus has already offered you his forgiveness. He paid the price for your sins when he died on the cross. There is nothing left for you to do but to believe and receive.

The Bible says, *"To all who did receive him, to those who believed in his name, he gave the right to become children of God."*[8] Believe Jesus died for your sins and God raised him from the dead, and receive his gift of forgiveness. There are no tests to pass, no hoops to jump through, and nothing to pay—the penalty for your sins has already been paid by Jesus Christ on the cross. Just receive his forgiveness by faith.

If you have never opened your heart to Jesus Christ, I invite you to pray this prayer right now:

Dear God, I know you created me. You made me to be loved by you and to love you back. Today,

I want to turn away from my plans and turn toward your will for my life. Please forgive me for my sins, for all the times I have turned away from you and acted like what you think doesn't matter. I'm amazed that you long for a relationship with me and that you're interested in the details of my life. But most of all, I'm amazed that you, Jesus, would come to earth to die for me and pay for my sin. I don't understand it all, but I say yes to you! Help me learn to love you and trust you and follow you in faith. From now on, I want to pursue your dream for my life. As much as I know how, I commit my life to you. In your name I pray. Amen.

If you just prayed that prayer, I would love to hear about it. Email me at Rick@PastorRick.com, and let me know about your decision to place your faith in Christ. I will send you material absolutely free to help you get started in your pursuit of God's dream for your life.

Reserve Time Alone with God

If you want to hear God's voice, then you have to silence the noise around you. The Bible says God speaks in a still, small voice, so you can't hear it in the whirlwind of a crazy life.

To visualize God's dream, you'll have to turn off the television and disconnect from your devices. You can't listen to God and binge-watch your favorite show at the same time. The reason you may never hear God speak to you could be that you're never quiet—there is always something going on. You have to reserve time alone with God so he can get a word in edgewise.

The Bible says in Job 37:14, *"Pause a moment . . . and listen; consider the wonderful things God does."*[9]

God wants to spend time with you. Amazing, isn't it? The creator of the universe says, "Pause, be quiet, and get alone with me so I can talk with you." This is the spiritual discipline of solitude. God speaks to people who take the time to listen. When was the last time you paused a moment to listen to God?

If you want to hear from God, you need to set aside time every day to read and study God's Word. During a quiet time, you pause, listen, and reflect on what God is doing in your life. It's a time when you talk to God in prayer and let God speak to you through the Bible. It's good to take time every day to do this. But it's also good to take an entire day at least once a year to be alone with God and to ask him, "Where do you want me to go, and what do you want me to do?" It's a day to pray, to think, to write, to set some goals and priorities, and to make course corrections to be sure you are pursuing God's dream for your life.

If you live to be seventy years old, you will live 25,567 days. Isn't it worth even one of those days to find out what God wants you to do with the rest of your life?

EVALUATE YOUR ABILITIES

You can discover God's will by looking at how he made you. What talents, abilities, experiences, spiritual gifts, and personality traits did he give you? These things are clues to the direction God wants you to go with your life. Why would he give you these gifts if he didn't intend for you to use them? That would be a waste.

The Bible says, *"God has given each of you some special abilities; be sure to use them to help each other."*[10] In other words, we are saved to serve. This is what ministry is all about—using your talents and gifts to help other people for God's glory.

Ephesians 2:10 says, *"We are God's handiwork,*

created in Christ Jesus to do good works, which God prepared in advance for us to do."[11] The Greek word translated "handiwork" is *poiema*, from which we get the word *poem*. There really is rhyme and reason to your life. You have a life message that you're meant to share with others. The New Living Translation says it this way: *"We are God's masterpiece."* You are a unique work of art, custom-made for a specific purpose. There is nobody exactly like you, and no one else can fulfill your purpose.

True fulfillment comes from being the person God meant you to be. So ask yourself, "What do I do well? What do I love to do? What am I passionate about? What energizes me and sets me in motion? What do others say I do well? What skills come naturally to me? What have been my most successful achievements? How can God use these abilities for his purposes?" You might want to set aside one full day to answer these questions. The answers will point the way to God's dream for your life.

ASSOCIATE WITH GODLY DREAMERS

Spend time with people who are trying to figure out God's dream for their own lives.

There is no such thing as a neutral friend. The

people you are closest to will either help you figure out God's dream or they'll hinder you, so choose your friends carefully. I've seen too many people miss God's dream because a close friend discouraged them.

Both dreams and discouragement are contagious. That's why it's important to be in a church family and surround yourself with people who are pursuing God's will. The Bible says, *"As iron sharpens iron, so a friend sharpens a friend,"*[12] and it also says, *"Bad company corrupts good character."*[13] If you want to follow God's dream for your life, then you need some godly friends who will help you discover it.

> **Both dreams and discouragement are contagious.**

At the same time, if you are married, part of your dream will involve your spouse (and children, if you have them). God will not give you a dream that ignores them so that you can just go off on your own. God's dream will be confirmed by the people closest to you.

MAKE YOUR DREAM PUBLIC

First, you visualize the dream. Then you verbalize the dream, saying, "This is what I believe God wants to do in my life." Announcing your dream to others demonstrates your faith and encourages people to be a part of God's plan.

Now, this isn't just theory. Let me tell you how this worked in my life. On March 30, 1980, I preached the first sermon at Saddleback Church. I was twenty-five years old. Standing before sixty people, I read the dream God had given me for our congregation:

It is a dream of a place where the hurting, the hopeless, the discouraged, the depressed, the frustrated, and the confused will find love, acceptance, help, forgiveness, guidance, encouragement, and support.

It is a dream of sharing the life-changing good news of Jesus Christ with hundreds of thousands of residents of South Orange County, California.

It is a dream of welcoming twenty thousand members into the fellowship of our church family—loving, learning, laughing, and living in harmony together, modeling God's love to the world.

It is a dream of growing people to spiritual maturity and their full potential through the discipleship of Bible studies, small groups, retreats, seminars, and tools to help them grow in Christlikeness and fulfill the purpose of their lives.

It is a dream of equipping every member for their own ministry through our church by helping them discover the gifts and talents God gave them.

It is a dream of sending out our members by the thousands on mission to every continent and empowering every member for their personal life mission in the world.

It is the dream of training church leaders and missionaries all around the world. It is the dream of starting at least one new daughter church every year.

It is a dream of at least fifty acres of land on which we will build a large regional church campus with beautiful yet efficient facilities, including a worship center seating thousands, a ministry center that provides a space for counseling and prayer, classrooms for Bible studies and training, and outdoor recreation areas. All these facilities will be designed to minister to the total person—spiritually, emotionally, physically, and socially—and they will be set in a natural park environment with inspiring garden landscapes that refreshes the soul, including beautiful flowers, green lawns and trees, picnic areas, sparkling fountains, and pools for baptizing. We want people to feel relaxed when they arrive.

Now, today, I stand before you and state with confident assurance that all these dreams will be realized. Why? Because they are inspired by God, and they are for his glory!

Today, all of it has come to pass, every single word and more. Only God could do that. Only God could have given me such an audacious dream. I went home scared to death. What had I done? Why didn't I just keep it a secret?

If I had kept this dream to myself, I might never have started and no one would have witnessed the miracle. The fear of failure could have kept me from doing what God wanted me to do.

There are three reasons for publicly stating your dream: First, it gets your dream off the ground. There can be no more procrastination. Once you've announced it, you're accountable to act on it and get moving.

The second reason is that it attracts other people's support. Why? Because a great dream inspires others to dream. The moment I stated my dream, other people wanted in on it. A dream from God may attract people you don't even know yet who will share their skills, resources, wisdom, passion, and energy to help you reach your goal.

The third reason for publicly stating your dream is that it releases God's power. In faith, you step out of the boat and start walking on water, and God holds you up. What you thought was impossible begins to come to pass. The Bible says, *"The one who calls you is faithful, and he will do it."*[14] Now that's a promise you can build your life on!

Start Dreaming

Once you discover God's dream for your life, you must arrange your entire life around that dream. Nothing is more important than fulfilling God's dream for you. It's the reason he created you. The apostle Paul said, *"I reckon my own life to be worth nothing to me; I only want to complete my mission and finish the work that the Lord Jesus gave me to do."*[15] The secret of greatness is having a single-minded focus.

That's what is needed in the world today: men and women of commitment, character, and conviction who are willing to put God's dream first in their lives. They are heroes for Christ. Extraordinary people are just ordinary people who attach themselves to extraordinary dreams.

Stop right now and ask yourself these questions: Why has God placed me on this earth? Why has God placed me in a particular area, with my particular passions and abilities, at this particular time in history? What could God do through my life if I gave it completely to him? The answers to those questions are where meaning, purpose, and significance are found.

> Nothing is more important than fulfilling God's dream for you. It's the reason he created you.

Nothing happens in your life until you start dreaming. I dare you to dream great dreams for God.

CHAPTER 3

Deciding to *Act*

If you are like that, unable to make up your mind and undecided in all you do, you must not think that you will receive anything from the Lord.

James 1:7–8 (GNT)

A dream is worthless until you wake up and act on it. You will never fulfill God's dream for your life until you press through the decision phase of faith.

The heroes of the Bible were bold decision makers:

- God gave Noah the dream of saving the world from the flood—but Noah had to make the decision to build the ark.
- God gave Abraham the dream of being the father of a great nation—but Abraham had to make the decision to leave the comfort and security of home and step out into the unknown.
- God gave Moses the dream of leading the children of Israel out of four hundred years of slavery—but Moses had to make the decision to confront Pharaoh.

- Jesus called the disciples to join him in ministry—but they had to make the decision to walk away from their careers to follow him.
- Jesus invited Peter to walk with him on the water—but Peter had to make the decision to get out of the boat and step into the miracle.

During the decision phase, you must do two things: First, you must invest. You have to decide to invest your time, your money, your reputation, and your energy in the things that will advance your pursuit of God's dream. You must stop making excuses and take the plunge. This is when you say, "God, I'm not going to procrastinate any longer. I'm going to do what you've told me to do."

The second thing you must do is let go of security. You can't move forward in faith while holding on to the past.

A great picture of letting go of security is a trapeze artist. She swings out on one bar and has to let go to grab the next bar and swing to the other side. The bars are far enough apart that she can't hold on to both at the same time. At some point she must let go of the security of the first bar, and for a split second she is flying in midair, holding on to neither one.

Have you ever been at the point in your career when you've left one job and you're looking for another, and there is nothing in between? It feels like you're a hundred feet in the air with no net below. But if you don't let go of your old life and grab on to the vision God wants for you, then you'll simply swing back in the old direction—only you won't swing all the way back. You'll just swing lower and lower until you finally stop, hanging there with only one way out: down.

Like the trapeze artist, you have to decide to let go of your security in order to take hold of your dream.

The decision phase is not about making quick decisions. It's about making the *right* decisions. Quick decisions are easy—that's why they're usually wrong. It takes a lot of wisdom to make the right decision. So I want to give you a simple, workable, biblical plan for making wise decisions. Whether it's your career, your education, your relationships, your finances, your health, your children, or your future, there are principles in God's Word that can help you make wise decisions. And each of

> The decision phase is not about making quick decisions. It's about making the *right* decisions.

these principles leads to a question that will guide
you toward God's dream.

Principle 1: Pray for Guidance

Before you do anything else, ask for God's perspective. The Bible says, *"If any of you need wisdom, you
should ask God, and it will be given to you."*[1] If it's
God's dream for you, it only makes sense to ask him
how to accomplish it.

Proverbs 28:26 says, *"A man is a fool to trust himself! But those who use God's wisdom are safe."*[2] Have
you ever made a foolish decision that you thought
was the best decision at the time? You need something greater than simple intuition or gut feelings.
You need absolute truth on which to base your decisions. You need God's guidance.

The Bible says, *"Blessed are those who find
wisdom, those who gain understanding."*[3] To find
wisdom, you must look for it. To gain understanding,
you must work for it. So how can you look for wisdom
and work for understanding?

First, read God's Word. Search the Scriptures.
Much of God's will for your life can be discovered in
the Bible. What has God already said that applies to

your situation? The more you know the Word of God, the better you will know the mind of God.

Second, listen to God's still, small voice whispering in your heart. God's voice is a voice of peace. The Bible says, *"The peace that Christ gives is to guide you in the decisions you make."*[4]

The fact is, God wants to guide you. He wants to help you in your decision-making. He wants you to succeed.

So ask, "What does God have to say about this decision?"

Principle 2: Get the Facts

There is no contradiction between faith and fact. It's wise to find out all you can before you make a decision. Proverbs 13:16 says, *"All who are prudent act with knowledge."*[5]

Before I started Saddleback Church, I spent six months scouting Orange County. I researched surveys and demographics. I studied the census. I wrote to pastors in the area. I conducted door-to-door interviews. After six months of study, I decided to pursue the dream.

Someone might ask, "Why did you do all that

extra work? Why didn't you just move in faith?" It's because the Bible says, *"What a shame—yes, how stupid!—to decide before knowing the facts!"*[6]

The reason many new businesses fail is because of uneducated enthusiasm. Somebody gets a "great idea" to start a business, but they don't get the facts. That's also why many marriages fail: uneducated enthusiasm. They think they're in love, but they don't face the facts. Their decision is based solely on feelings.

So what's the solution? The solution is to ask, "What do I need to know before I make this decision?" Then do what you need to do to get the facts.

Principle 3: Ask for Advice

Talk to somebody who's made a similar decision. Talk to friends who know your strengths and weaknesses. Seek wise counsel and prayer support from people who know God's Word and who aren't afraid to tell you the truth. Proverbs 24:6 says, *"The more good advice you get, the more likely you are to win."*[7]

You can also look to the Bible for wise advice. Romans 15:4 says, *"Everything that was written in the past was written to teach us."*[8] The Bible is filled with stories of real people who've learned incredible life lessons—both good and bad. Take Jonah, for example. He was someone who knew God's plan but decided to run away from it. And even though Jonah made a few mistakes, he also did a few things right. The good news is, we can learn from both the good and bad experiences of Jonah's life.

It is wise to learn from experience, but it's wiser to learn from the experiences of others. I don't have time to learn everything from personal experience. I don't have time to make all the mistakes in life, and you don't either. You can learn from others' successes, and you can learn from others' failures. If you're wise, you won't try to learn everything firsthand. You will ask for advice and learn from the experiences of others. And believe me, it's a lot less painful that way.

The problem is that we often would rather *appear* wise than *be* wise. We think that if we ask for advice, we'll look like a fool. But the Bible says wise people ask for advice. Humility and wisdom go hand in hand. If you won't ask for advice, then you've got an ego problem. The Bible says, *"[Arrogant people's] hearts are dull and stupid."*[9]

> The problem is that we often would rather *appear* wise than *be* wise.

They are stupid because they're unwilling to be teachable.

If you won't learn from other people, you will never succeed in life. Proverbs 20:18 says, *"Get good advice and you will succeed; don't go charging into battle without a plan."*[10]

One of the best places to learn from others and find godly dreamers is at your local church. If you're not connected to a church, you can find one. There are likely many good churches in your area. If not, you can join one online. There's no such thing as a solitary Christian. You need a church family.

So humble yourself and ask, "Who can I talk to and ask for advice?"

Principle 4: Calculate the Cost

Every decision has a price tag. It will cost you time, money, energy, reputation, talent, and resources. There is always an investment to be made. The Bible says in Proverbs 20:25, *"It is a trap to dedicate something rashly and only later to consider one's vows."*[11] It's a trap to decide without deliberating, to promise without pondering, to commit without first considering the cost.

When people pressure you to make a decision, it's okay to say, "I'll get back to you." It's not as important to make a quick decision as it is to make the *right* decision—and the right decision has to be an informed decision.

Here is a law of life: it's easier to get in than it is to get out. Is it easier to get into debt than to get out of debt? Is it easier to get into a relationship than to get out of a relationship? Is it easier to fill up your schedule than it is to fulfill your schedule? You bet it is. Because of that, you have to calculate the cost.

Jesus said, *"Don't begin until you count the cost. For who would begin construction of a building without first calculating the cost to see if there is enough money to finish it? . . . Or what king would go to war against another king without first sitting down with his counselors to discuss whether his army of 10,000 could defeat the 20,000 soldiers marching against him?"*[12]

Every decision has a price tag. You have to ask, "Is it worth it?"

Principle 5: Prepare for Problems

You may remember Murphy's Law: "Anything that can go wrong *will* go wrong." Problems are inevitable.

They are part of life! Even Jesus said, *"In this world you will have trouble."*[13] You can't ignore problems because problems will not ignore you. Instead, you have to prepare for them. The Bible says, *"A prudent man foresees the difficulties ahead and prepares for them."*[14]

In the process of preparation, expect the best, but prepare for the worst. Expect God to lead you as you pursue his dream. But also prepare for the problems that are coming. Every good idea has something wrong with it. That doesn't mean you shouldn't do it; it just means you need to be aware and prepare.

In Proverbs 27:12, King Solomon said the same thing: *"A sensible man watches for problems ahead and prepares to meet them. The simpleton never looks and suffers the consequences."*[15] The wise person knows there are problems with every decision and prepares for them.

There's a big difference between preparing for a problem and solving a problem. Never confuse decision-making with problem-solving. They are two different things. If you have to solve all the problems before you make a decision, then you'll never get anywhere. In the decision phase of faith, you prepare for the problems, but you don't try to solve them all ahead of time.

When President Kennedy announced in 1961 that the United States would land a man on the moon by the end of the decade, the technology needed to get there didn't exist. Some of it hadn't even been thought of! NASA calculated the risks and prepared for the problems, but they didn't solve all the problems before the decision was made. Once the decision was made, then they started solving the problems.

> **Never confuse decision-making with problem-solving.**

When my wife, Kay, and I started Saddleback Church, we had no money, no members, and no building—but we didn't let that stop us. We were aware of the problems, but we didn't solve all of them before we started.

The Bible says, *"If you wait for perfect conditions, you will never get anything done."*[16] Perfectionism is the enemy of progress. It produces procrastination. It paralyzes potential. Face the truth, friend: perfect conditions are never going to come. There will always be a reason to say no. But just because you have a reason to say no doesn't mean it's not the season to say yes.

If there were no reason to say no, then you wouldn't need any faith—and without faith, it is impossible to please God. God provides as the needs arise. He wants you to depend on him. Don't try to solve all the problems up front. Answers start coming once you start moving.

So ask, "What could go wrong, and will I be ready if it does?"

Principle 6: Face Your Fears

Fear is at the root of all indecision: fear that you will make a mistake, that you'll fail, that you'll embarrass yourself; fear that you will make a commitment you can't keep, that somebody will laugh at you or reject you, that God's dream for your life will never become reality. It's always fear that keeps us from being decisive.

We don't like to admit we're afraid, so we make excuses:

- Abraham said, "I'm too old."
- Moses said, "I can't talk."
- Gideon said, "I can't fight."
- Isaiah said, "I'm too sinful."
- Jeremiah said, "I'm too young."

What's your excuse?

God has a dream for your life. You may be saying, "I don't have the time, I don't have the money, I don't have the experience, I don't have the education, I don't have the contacts, I don't have the resources. If only I were married. If only I were *not* married! If only I were older. If only I were younger." It's fear that's keeping you from making the decision God wants you to make.

God has always used imperfect people in imperfect situations to accomplish his perfect will. If you're waiting for that perfect person to come along, I have news for you: They're not coming. They don't exist! If you're waiting for the perfect situation, for things to be just right, or for certain things to be finished before you really commit your life to Christ, it's not going to happen. The basic commitments of life must be made in the middle of the stuff of life. Life goes on.

What's the antidote to fear? Faith. Romans 8:31 says, *"If God is for us, who can be against us?"*[17] Trust God, and start moving toward your dream in spite of the problems, fears, or doubts. The secret to getting unstuck is to move against your fear and do the thing you fear most.

If God has given you a dream and you know it's his will, then make the decision and move against your fear. Watch the Red Sea open up! Watch the walls fall down! Watch the stone roll away from the tomb! Watch God work a miracle in your life.

When I don't have the faith to do something, I go ahead and do it anyway, as though I had the faith. Then the faith comes. A little faith in a big God gets big results.

So ask, "What am I afraid of?"

Make the Decision

You have a decision to make. The truth is, not to decide *is* to decide. You are the sum total of your choices. Your choices define your character. You must determine what you are committed to and what decisions you need to make. God won't force you to make a decision, and he won't make the decision for you. He has given you freedom to choose.

I implore you: Do something great with your life for Jesus's sake! Don't waste your life. Don't live in mediocrity. Don't just exist. Make the decisions that will determine your destiny.

CHAPTER 4

Persisting through *Delays*

These things I plan won't happen right away.
Slowly, steadily, surely, the time approaches
when the vision will be fulfilled.

Habakkuk 2:3 (TLB)

Are you stuck in God's waiting room?

Dreams are never fulfilled immediately. Have you ever wondered why God waits to answer your prayer? If he hears you and has the power to answer, why does he delay? There is almost always a waiting period when you're following God in faith.

- Noah waited 120 years from the time he started building the ark until it began to rain.
- Abraham waited 100 years for his promised son, Isaac, to be born.
- Joseph spent years in prison waiting for God to fulfill his destiny.
- Daniel waited seventy years to see his people return to Jerusalem from their captivity in Babylon.
- Even Jesus waited thirty years in a carpenter's shop before starting his ministry.

There is always a delay.

The classic story of delay is the children of Israel, who were brought out of Egypt by God and then wandered around the desert for forty years before they entered the promised land. It's only about a two-week walk from Egypt to Israel. It took them forty years to get there. What in the world were they doing? What in the world was God doing?

The Bible says this about their delay: "*When Pharaoh finally let the people go, God did not lead them along the main road that runs through Philistine territory, even though that was the shortest route to the Promised Land. God said, 'If the people are faced with a battle, they might change their minds and return to Egypt.' So God led them in a roundabout way through the wilderness toward the Red Sea.*"[1]

God's people were delayed by design. God knew if they went to war, they wouldn't be able to handle it. So he led them the long way to the Red Sea. Then, after they miraculously crossed the Red Sea, God had them wander around the wilderness for forty years.

Why does God cause delays? Well, for three reasons. Sometimes God uses delays to protect us *from* difficulties. Sometimes he uses them to prepare us *for* difficulties. And sometimes he uses delays to develop us *in* difficulties. The Bible says, *"The Lord led you through the wilderness for all those forty years . . . testing you to find out how you would respond, and whether or not you would really obey him."*[2]

How you respond to God's delays is a test of your maturity. God is growing you up while you're waiting. It takes as little as six hours to grow a mushroom. It takes sixty years to grow a mature oak tree. So what do you want to be when you grow up—a mushroom or an oak tree? James 1:4 says, *"Let the process go on until that endurance is fully developed, and you will find you have become [a person] of mature character."*[3]

When you're sitting in one of God's waiting rooms, there are four things you should not do because they will only prolong the delay: don't fear, don't fret, don't faint, and don't forget. These are attitudes of unbelief.

Don't Fear

There are many reasons for the delays in life, but fear is our own fault. God led his people to the bank of the Jordan River and said, "There it is! The promised land! It's yours for the taking." But the Bible says they would not enter the land because they were afraid of the people who lived there. They were delayed because they were afraid.

Fear of other people is one of the biggest barriers to fulfilling God's dream. The Bible says, *"Fear of man is a dangerous trap, but to trust in God means safety."*[4] The Israelites had enough faith to move out of Egypt, but they didn't have enough faith to move into the promised land. And because of their fear, they were trapped in the wilderness. They were delayed because they were afraid, and God made them wait forty more years in the desert.

Are you trapped in a wilderness because of your fear of other people's resistance? Are you so preoccupied with their opinions that you can't occupy your promised land? The problem with fear is that it keeps you in the wilderness. Fear prolongs the delay. Perhaps many of your dreams have never been fulfilled, not because of God but because of *you*—you won't step out in faith. You think you're waiting on God, but God is waiting on you.

When you're afraid to go after the dream God has given you, you need to focus on God's presence because when he is with you, it doesn't matter who is against you (Romans 8:31). Isaiah 41:10 says, *"Fear not, for I am with you; be not be dismayed, for I am your God; I will strengthen you, I will help you, I will uphold you."*[5] God has not for-gotten you. He has promised, *"I will never leave you; I will never abandon you."*[6] That

Fear prolongs the delay.

means there will never be a time when God is not with you. He's with you right now. He's with you on your good days and on your bad days. He's with you when you feel his presence and when you don't. God says, "I will always be with you." When God is near, there is nothing to fear. So don't fear! Instead, focus on God's presence. He is with you all the time.

You might be in the middle of a delay right now. You've been praying about something, but it hasn't happened yet. You're wondering if God has forgotten you. But God has not forgotten you, and you are not alone. It is a delay by design. God knows what you're going through. He wants to build your character, and he wants you to learn to trust him. You can count on God to help.

There are 365 "fear not" statements in the Bible. That's one for every day of the year! God wants you to get the message: don't be afraid. The answer to your prayer is coming. Just hang on.

Don't Fret

I'm convinced there is a sign in God's waiting room that says, "Stop fretting, and start trusting." Aren't you glad God understands us? He knows our tendency to worry. He knows that when things take too long, we start stressing and griping—which is what the Israelites did.

"On the way the people lost their patience and spoke against God and Moses. They complained, 'Why did you bring us out of Egypt to die in this desert, where there is no food or water? We can't stand any more of this miserable food!'"[7]

Fretting was one of the sins that kept the Israelites out of the promised land. They worried and griped all the time, no matter what God did for them. They complained about the journey. They complained about the delay. They complained about the leadership. They complained when there was no water, so God provided water. Then they complained that there was no food, so God provided food. Then they complained about the food he gave them! Like the Israelites, it's so easy for us to gripe when we're forced to wait.

But worrying is a waste of time. It's fretting

without fixing. It's stewing without doing. Worrying is like sitting in a rocking chair. You expend a lot of energy, but you don't get anywhere. You just go back and forth, back and forth . . . should I or shouldn't I . . . will he or won't he . . . are they or aren't they . . . back and forth, back and forth, with absolutely no progress.

The Bible says, *"Rest in the Lord; wait patiently for him to act . . . Don't fret and worry—it only leads to harm."*[8] God doesn't want you to fret and get uptight. He wants you to stay calm. Fretting is a response to fear, but resting is an act of faith.

It's frustrating to be in a hurry when God isn't— and God is never in a hurry. He is never late, and he is never early either. He is always right on time. God doesn't need your help to speed things along, but he does want your cooperation, and he wants you to trust his timing. The Bible says in Ecclesiastes 3:11, *"He has set the right time for everything."*[9] God's timing is perfect!

So instead of worrying, the Bible says, *"Fix your thoughts on what is true and good and right. Think about things that are pure and lovely, and dwell on the fine, good things in others. Think about all you can praise God for and be glad about. . . . And the God of peace will be with you."*[10] When you spend time thinking about the things God loves, you will experience his peace.

Don't Faint

When you go through delays in life, don't get discouraged. Don't lose heart or give up on your dream. Instead, wait on God. Isaiah 40:31 says, *"They that wait upon the Lord shall renew their strength. They shall mount up with wings like eagles; they shall run and not be weary; they shall walk and not faint."*[11] Who are those who do not faint? They're those who wait on the Lord.

This is the third thing that kept the Israelites out of the promised land: they didn't wait on the Lord for strength. The Bible says, *"All the Israelites grumbled against Moses. . . . 'If only we had died in Egypt! . . . We should choose a leader and go back to Egypt.'"*[12] Nothing depletes your strength quicker than grumbling and complaining.

"If only" and "go back" are telltale signs of discouragement: "If only I had stayed where I was. If only I'd done *this* or *that*." When we look back, we start second-guessing ourselves: "Maybe I didn't really hear from God. Maybe I just made this up. Maybe God isn't listening. Maybe he doesn't care." And then we start to idealize the past: "Let's go back to 'Egypt'—the good old days." The problem with the good old days is that they weren't really all that good. Most of the time, the only good thing about them is that they are over. The good old days usually look better in hindsight than they really were. We easily forget about old difficulties when we're faced with new challenges.

The Israelites had lived in slavery in Egypt for four hundred years, and now they wanted to go back. Some people would rather live in slavery to their past than face the fear of freedom. They aren't willing to push through and work on the problem. They want to give up and go back. They settle for mediocrity in life. They settle for less than God's best.

Instead of fainting or giving up, be persistent and pray. God told Joshua to march around the walls of Jericho, and the walls would fall down. But it didn't happen on the first try. The Israelites had to march around the city seven days in a row, and on the seventh day they had to march seven more times. Why the delay? Why didn't the walls fall the first time? God was teaching his people to be persistent and pray.

The Bible says, *"Let us not be weary in well doing: for in due season we shall reap, if we faint not."*[13]

There is always a delay between sowing and reaping. You plant in one season and reap in another. God wants to see if you're going to keep cultivating, planting, and sowing while you wait for the dream to come to fruition. He wants to see if you really mean business. If God sees consistency in your life, then the harvest comes—but it will not come immediately. Why? If there is no delay, then there is no character development and no stretching of your faith.

> There is always a delay between sowing and reaping.

Jesus told us that we *"must always pray and never lose heart."*[14] "Always pray" and "lose heart" are the two options you have in life. You will either do one or the other. If you pray continually, you will not lose heart, but if you don't pray continually, you will lose heart. You have to pray for persistence and persist prayerfully.

In this third phase, delay, you always have to make a choice: "Will I panic or pray?" Praying, "Lord, help me hold on and not give up," helps you to not fear, fret, or faint.

Don't Forget

The longer the delay, the shorter our memory becomes. When there is a delay, we tend to forget our dream. We forget God's goodness to us in the past. We forget that God is with us. We forget God's power. We start focusing on all our problems instead of what God has done for us.

This was the Israelites' fourth mistake in the wilderness. The Bible tells us, *"They forgot the many times [God] showed them his love, and they rebelled against the Almighty at the Red Sea. But he saved them, as he had promised. . . . But they soon forgot all he had done; they had no patience for his plan."*[15] Notice this passage says they forgot the "many times" God had blessed them.

It's unbelievable how short their memory was. God sent ten plagues to Egypt to secure the Israelites' freedom, but they forgot all about it just a few days later when they thought they would die at the Red Sea. Then, God miraculously opened the Red Sea, and they crossed it on dry land, but they forgot all about it just a few days later when they thought they would die of thirst. Then, God miraculously provided water in the desert, but they forgot all about it just a few days later when they thought they would die of starvation. They were constantly forgetting what God had done for them.

We shouldn't be too quick to judge the Israelites because we do the same thing. When a delay occurs, we start acting like God has never done anything for us. Has God done good things for you in the past? Sure he has—and you can count on him to do them again. But when you act like God is not going to bail you out of a new problem, you're forgetting all the other times he's come to your rescue.

Psalm 103:2 says, *"I will bless the Lord and not forget the glorious things he does for me."*[16] What have you forgotten about God's goodness? How has he helped you in the past? Before you move on to the next chapter of this book, I want you to get a piece of paper and write down everything God has already done for you. Think about it: What prayers has he answered? What needs has he met? What difficulties has he helped you overcome? Write them down. I guarantee they will build your faith for whatever you are facing today.

In the Waiting

If you think God is taking too long to fulfill your dream, remember that the Bible says, *"The Lord is not being slow in carrying out his promises. . . . Rather is he being patient with you."*[17] Certainly, God can do things immediately, but he's working on a larger agenda. He wants you to learn a lesson before he brings the solution. He wants to develop you before he delivers you.

You may think you're ready, but God knows you aren't. Waiting keeps you from getting ahead of God. Waiting teaches you to trust him. It teaches you that his timing is perfect and that you are not in control.

God is never in a hurry. The delays that come into your life do not defeat God's purpose. They *fulfill* God's purpose. They make you a better person—they make you more like Jesus Christ.

So what have you been waiting on God to do? Are you waiting for him to turn a problem around? To answer a prayer? To make a way in a place where it seems impossible for there to be a way—financially, physically, relationally, or vocationally? Maybe you've been waiting on God to bring that right person along. Maybe you've been waiting on God to turn a crisis into a victory. God has not forgotten you. A delay is not a denial.

There's a big difference between "No" and "Not yet." Many times, God says, "Not yet," but we think he's saying, "No." That's why the most common reaction in the delay phase is doubt. We start thinking, "Maybe I missed God's vision. Maybe God changed his mind. Maybe I did something wrong." But again, a delay is not a denial. A delay never destroys God's purpose in your life.

A delay is not a denial.

The Bible says, *"These things I plan won't happen right away. Slowly, steadily, surely, the time approaches when the vision will be fulfilled. If it seems slow, do not despair, for these things will surely come to pass. Just be patient! They will not be overdue a single day!"*[18]

God will fulfill his purpose in your life if you do not fear, do not fret, do not faint, and do not forget.

CHAPTER 5

Dealing with
Difficulties

In this world you will have trouble.
But take heart! I have overcome the world.

John 16:33 (NIV)

Every trial is a teacher. Every storm is a school. Every experience is an education. Every difficulty is for your development.

Let's review the phases of faith we've covered so far: In phase one, God gives you a dream of what he wants to do with your life. In phase two, you decide to go for the dream. Then, along comes phase three, the inevitable delay. And just when you think you can't wait any longer, you run into phase four: difficulty.

Jesus told us this would happen. In John 16:33, he said, *"In this world you will have trouble. But take heart! I have overcome the world."*[1] Trouble is a part of life. The question is not if you will have difficulties. The question is how you will respond to them. Your response reveals your emotional and spiritual maturity.

Few people have faced the difficulties the apostle Paul experienced. Here's what he said about his troubles:

I've worked much harder, been jailed more often, beaten up more times than I can count, and at death's door time after time. I've been flogged five times with the Jews' thirty-nine lashes, beaten by Roman rods three times, pummeled with rocks once. I've been shipwrecked three times, and immersed in the open sea for a night and a day. In hard traveling year in and year out, I've had to ford rivers, fend off robbers, struggle with friends, struggle with foes. I've been at risk in the city, at risk in the country, endangered by desert sun and sea storm, and betrayed by those I thought were my brothers. I've known drudgery and hard labor, many a long and lonely night without sleep, many a missed meal, blasted by the cold, naked to the weather. And that's not the half of it, when you throw in the daily pressures and anxieties of all the churches.[2]

In spite of all the trouble Paul experienced throughout his ministry, he never gave up on God's dream for his life. He had a much greater perspective. Paul wrote, *"We're not giving up. How could we! Even though on the outside it often looks like things are falling apart on us, on the inside, where God is making new life, not a day goes by without his unfolding grace."*[3] He went on to say in 2 Corinthians 6:4, *"In everything we do we show that we are God's servants by patiently enduring troubles, hardships, and difficulties."*[4] Patient endurance is the key to success.

One of the greatest difficulties in Paul's life is described in Acts 27. Paul was being taken by ship to Rome as a prisoner. He warned the captain and crew not to sail out of the harbor because God had told him there would be a storm. The captain grew impatient and decided to leave anyway, and they sailed right into disaster.

The crew made three common mistakes when they decided to set sail. They are the same mistakes you and I make that often get us into trouble.

First, they listened to bad advice. Acts 27:11 says, *"[They] followed the advice of the pilot."*[5] God had already told them not to go, but because the "expert" said it was okay, they set sail. There are a lot of experts in the world. They are on every talk show and news feed. But if God tells you to do something and all the experts in the world contradict his word, don't listen to the experts. Listen to what God says.

The crew's second mistake was that they followed the crowd. They gave in to peer pressure. There were 276 people onboard the ship. Verse 12 says, *"The majority decided that we should sail."*[6] A phrase you'll commonly hear is, "But everybody's doing it." So what? The majority is often wrong. Lemmings are small rodents that have been known to follow each other over a cliff and drown in the ocean. Whole pods of whales have been known to beach themselves. If everybody is doing it, maybe nobody is thinking. If God says no or tells you to go another way, then he is the only one you need to follow.

Their third mistake was that they relied on circumstances. Verse 13 says, *"When a gentle south wind began to blow, they saw their opportunity."*[7] The crew thought it was a nice day for sailing. But circumstances aren't always as they appear. Even though it looked okay for them to sail out into the ocean, God had already said no—and they soon headed right into a storm.

You should not go through every open door you see. You should not take advantage of every opportunity that comes your way. You should not accept every job offer given to you. You should not date everybody who asks you out. With any opportunity, you need to ask if it is what God wants.

With any opportunity, you need to ask if it is what God wants.

Have you experienced a shipwreck in your life? Perhaps you've been through an emotional shipwreck. Maybe you've had a relational shipwreck. Have you been through a shipwreck in your finances or career or health? What are you supposed to do when you face those kinds of difficulties?

In Acts 27 we learn three things to do when dealing with difficulties: determine the reason, determine the result, and determine our response.

Determine the Reason

Ask: "What caused this trouble?"

There are only four causes for difficulty in our lives: First, there's *us*, which means we need to acknowledge, "I'm the first and greatest cause of my troubles." I know it's hard for us to admit, but it's true that we bring most of our problems on ourselves. The second cause is other people. The third cause is the devil. And the fourth cause is God. That's right: God can cause difficulty in our lives. He allows problems to come into our lives to get our attention, to test us, and to mold our character.

The most difficult type of trouble to deal with is when you're the innocent victim. Not every shipwreck in your life is your fault. Sometimes you're simply in the wrong place at the wrong time. Paul was a prisoner; he had no choice. He experienced a shipwreck because of other people's poor decisions.

When you're going through a tough time, how do you know what the source of it is? You must pray about it and ask the Lord to show you. The Bible says, *"I tried to think this problem through, but it was too difficult for me until I went into your Temple."*[8] When you worship God, he brings clarity to your life. He opens your eyes to see things the way he sees them.

So first, determine the reason and ask, "What caused this problem? Was it me? Was it other people? Was it the devil? Or was it God?"

Determine the Result

Ask: "What does God want me to learn from this difficulty?"

Paul wrote in Romans 5:3–4, *"We can rejoice, too, when we run into problems and trials, for we know that they are good for us—they help us learn to be patient. And patience develops strength of character in us and helps us trust God more each time.*"[9] God wants to teach you through your troubles. He wants to develop your character through your crises.

The problem is that most of us are slow learners. We usually miss the lesson the first time, so God allows us to experience the same difficulties over and over. He does this because he is more interested in your character than your comfort. God is more interested in making you like Christ than he is in making things easy for you.

You might be facing a major difficulty, even a shipwreck, right now. It may be an illness, a fear, a financial problem, or a strain in a relationship. What result is God looking for? What do you think he's trying to teach you? As Paul said, God wants you to develop strength of character, and he wants you to learn to trust him. God doesn't want you to give up on the dream; he wants you to grow up into the likeness of Jesus Christ.

Determine My Response

Ask: "How should I respond to my trouble?"

Life isn't fair, and sometimes it hurts—that's a given. But how we respond is entirely up to us. We will become either better or bitter. We will either grow up or give up. We will either become what God wants us to be or we will shrivel, and our hearts will become hard. It's our choice.

What happens *to* you is not nearly as important as what happens *in* you. Why? Because what happens to you is temporary, but what happens in you is eternal. It's all about your character because your character is the only thing you will take with you into eternity.

> What happens *to* you is not nearly as important as what happens *in* you.

So how should you respond when difficulties come your way? Paul's story in Acts 27 teaches us three things we should not do and three things we should do when we find ourselves in one of life's storms. Here are three things we should *not* do.

Don't Drift

Acts 27:15 says, *"The ship was caught by the storm and could not head into the wind; so we gave way to it and were driven along."*[10] The ship was in the middle of the Mediterranean Sea. The sailors hadn't seen the sun or stars for fourteen days. Because they couldn't get their bearings, they had no idea where they were. So they gave up hope of reaching their destination and just started drifting.

That's what happens to people who lose sight of their goal, their purpose, their dream for their life: They drift on a sea of uncertainty. They just go along to get along. We don't call it drifting today; we call it coasting. The problem with coasting is that you only pick up speed when you're headed downhill.

Don't lose sight of your dream when life gets hard. Stay focused on your goal and what God is teaching you, and remember he has not left you to pursue your dream alone.

Don't Discard

Acts 27:18 says, *"They began to throw the cargo overboard."*[11] They were battered so badly by the wind and waves that the crew started throwing things overboard to lighten the ship. First, they threw the cargo overboard, then they threw the tackle overboard, and then the grain. They discarded things they needed because the storm was so tough. But a lightened load did not lessen the storm.

This is a common reaction to difficulty. When the pressure comes and the stress is unbearable, we begin to let go of what is truly valuable. We say, "I'm throwing in the towel. I'm giving up on my family. I'm abandoning this business. I'm letting go of my dream." We start throwing out things we shouldn't throw out. We compromise our values, forget our heritage, and give up on relationships.

Some of the sailors attempted to abandon ship. But in Acts 27:31, Paul told the centurion, *"Unless these men stay with the ship, you cannot be saved."*[12] So the soldiers cut the ropes to the lifeboats and let them fall away. With no other means of escape, everyone was forced to stay with the ship. God would not let them run. They had to ride out the storm.

Have you done that in your marriage? Have you cut the lifeboats loose so there's no way out? Have you said, "Divorce is not an option for us; we're going to make this marriage work"? If you haven't, you will often be tempted to jump ship.

If you don't cut the ropes to the lifeboats, you'll never develop the character God wants you to have. It is always easier to cop out than it is to develop character. God can change situations and personalities. He can even change you! But he won't if you're always running away. God says, "Stay with the ship." Don't discard the values you know are right and important.

Don't Despair

Acts 27:20 says, *"When neither sun nor stars appeared for many days and the storm continued raging, we finally gave up all hope of being saved."*[13] Hope is always the last thing to go. Paul and the crew had been in total darkness for fourteen days. They had no idea where they were going. They were being tossed back and forth by uncontrollable forces. They gave up their cargo, their tackle, and their food. Finally, they gave up hope.

But they had forgotten one thing: even in a storm, God is in control. He hadn't left them—and he hasn't left you. Don't despair. You may not feel his presence, but he is with you in your storm. He will help you through it. God is testing you to see if you will trust him.

The apostle Paul had the right perspective about all the difficulties he faced. He said, *"We do not lose heart. Though outwardly we are wasting away, yet inwardly we are being renewed day by day. For our light and momentary troubles are achieving for us an eternal glory that far outweighs them all."*[14] After all he went through, after all he suffered, Paul knew that compared with the glory awaiting him in heaven, it was all "light and

Troubles don't come to stay; they come to pass.

83

momentary." His faith was unconquerable. He knew that troubles don't come to stay; they come to pass.

So, then, what is the right response to difficulty? Here are three things we *should* do.

Confess My Part

If you brought the trouble on yourself, admit it. Stop blaming other people. Stop making excuses. If you have a problem with addiction, admit it. If you have a problem with your temper or your tongue, admit it. If you have a problem with your spending, admit it. Jesus said when you know the truth, *"the truth will set you free."*[15] But it's only the truth you know—the truth you face—that will bring freedom.

What are you pretending is not a problem and is getting in the way of fulfilling your dream? The Bible says, *"A man who refuses to admit his mistakes can never be successful. But if he confesses and forsakes them, he gets another chance."*[16] Do you want another chance? Then confess your part in the problem and accept responsibility.

Confront It

The only way to face a storm is head-on. Don't run from it. Don't try to go under it, over it, or around it. You have to confront it. You will never solve a problem by ignoring it.

God won't take you around the storm. He will take you *through* the storm. If you turn sideways, you'll capsize. God wants you to face the storm, not fear it. Face the conflict in your relationship. Face the conflict with your health. Face the conflict with your work. You will never recognize the miracle until you recognize the impossibility. God never said it would be easy, but he promises, "I will be with you." You are going to make it!

Claim a Promise

When you face a problem, find a promise. There are more than seven thousand promises in the Bible that you can claim when you're going through tough times. You can overcome discouragement when you stop focusing on what could go wrong and start focusing on God's promises.

Everything was falling apart in the storm—except Paul. Why wasn't Paul falling apart? Because his confidence was in God, not in the ship. Paul was clinging to God's promise. In Acts 27:25, Paul said, *"Keep up your courage, men, for I have faith in God that it will happen just as he told me."*[17] Paul knew

God would keep his promises. God didn't say the ship would make it. Rather, he said it would break apart. But God did say the men would make it—and they did, some by swimming to shore and others by floating on pieces of the ship.

You may be going through a storm right now. Your ship may not make it. You may lose the house. You may lose the car. You may lose the job. God never promised to keep all your comforts around you. But he did say you would make it. You may have to dog paddle. You may have to get to shore on a broken piece of the ship. But you're going to make it.

None of us have completely whole lives; we are all broken people. You may have a broken heart. You may have a broken home. But if you hold on to God's promises, you will make it.

Don't Give Up

Is a storm threatening your ship? Do you feel bashed and battered? Do you feel like that ship in the Mediterranean, lost in the dark and ready to fall apart? Are difficulties delaying the dream? You're in phase four. Don't give up—look up! Don't become anxious and afraid. Don't allow yourself to drift or let go of your dream. Don't discard the values and relationships that you know are important. Don't throw away your convictions. Don't despair and let go of God, because he has promised, *"I will never leave you nor forsake you."*[18]

Don't drift, don't discard, don't despair—and never, ever give up hope. God's purpose is greater than your problems.

CHAPTER 6

Facing Dead *Ends*

What is impossible with man
is possible with God.
Luke 18:27 (NIV)

Cancer. Divorce. Foreclosure. Bankruptcy. Infertility. Unemployment. These are dead-end words—individual words that sound more like a sentence. They instill fear and hopelessness, and they can turn your dream to dust.

So how do you respond when your dream becomes a nightmare? What do you do when life is out of control? Do you doubt God's love and wisdom? Do you question his character? Do you wonder if he is some kind of cruel joker who gives you a dream only to crush it? If you do, then you have reached phase five of faith: the dead-end phase.

In the dead-end phase, you start asking, "What's going on, God? Did I miss your will? Have I missed your vision? Is this just something I thought up myself?"

Moses's Dead End

The best example of a dead end is when Moses led the Israelites out of Egypt. After God sent ten plagues to punish the Egyptians for holding his people in slavery, Pharaoh finally said, *"Get out! . . . And take the rest of the Israelites with you!"*[1] But soon after, Pharaoh changed his mind and sent his army to pursue the Israelites to bring them back.

The Israelites were trapped at the Red Sea, with mountains on each side, the sea in front of them, and the enemy army bearing down on them. There was no way out—and that's exactly where God wanted them.

The Bible says the people were terrified and complained that they should have remained as slaves in Egypt rather than die at the Red Sea. Some people, even today, would rather live in bondage than take a risk for freedom. They'll put up with a bad situation that is not God's will rather than pursue God's plan and trust him for a miracle.

Perhaps you feel like your enemy, Satan, is in hot pursuit to drag you back into addiction, back into despair, or back into old habits that enslaved you. He whispers in your ear, "I told you so. You'll never be free. Your life will never amount to anything. Your 'dream' is just a hallucination. Who do you think you are?"

But "Who do you think you are?" is the wrong

question. The right question to answer is, "Who do you think God is?"

Why were the Israelites at the Red Sea? Because God led them there—and he led them there for a purpose. Though the people thought they were doomed, God had a surprise in store. He was about to display his power like never before.

Moses said, *"Do not be afraid. Stand firm and you will see the deliverance the LORD will bring you today. The Egyptians you see today you will never see again. The LORD will fight for you; you need only to be still."*[2]

Is your back against the wall? Do you wish you had never started moving toward God's dream? Are the odds stacked against you? Then it's time to stand firm and look for God's protection and provision—even when you can't see it. The Bible says, *"If you do not stand firm in your faith, you will not stand at all."*[3]

The Israelites were at a dead end, but deliverance was coming.

Abraham's Dead End

Abraham also reached the fifth phase of faith. God had given him the dream of being the father of a great nation. At ninety-nine years old, Abraham and his barren wife, Sarah, still had no children of their own. Then when Abraham was one hundred, miraculously, Isaac, the promised child, was born. But in Genesis 22, God asks Abraham to give up his son. God said, *"Take your son, your only son, whom you love—Isaac—and go to the region of Moriah. Sacrifice him there as a burnt offering on a mountain I will show you."*[4]

What God told Abraham to do may be unsettling, but God was testing Abraham. It seemed Abraham's dream for the future was being taken away. Abraham had reached a dead end. But he continued to do what God told him to do, knowing that God would provide a way out. The Bible tells us, *"[Abraham] believed that if Isaac died God would bring him back to life again."*[5]

You might be at a dead end today. Perhaps you're asking, "Why is this happening to me?" It's because God is getting you ready for phase six, the deliverance phase of faith. God is preparing you for a miracle. The darker your situation, the more despairing your circumstance, and the more hopeless things may seem, the more God is preparing you for an even greater deliverance.

What should you do when you come to a dead end and you're waiting for your deliverance to come?

In Romans 4, Paul teaches us four lessons we can learn from Abraham while he was waiting for deliverance.

Remember What God Can Do

The situation may be out of your control, but it is not out of God's control. When you face a dead end, don't focus on what you *can't* do; focus on what God *can* do. The Bible says, *"Abraham believed [in] God who gives life to the dead and who creates something out of nothing."*[6]

Only God can give life to the dead. Only God can create something out of nothing. That's the definition of a miracle. If God can give life to a dead human being, he can give life to a dead

> When you face a dead end, don't focus on what you *can't* do; focus on what God *can* do.

career. He can give life to a dead marriage. He can give life to a dead dream. He can break through a financial dead end. He can make a way where there is no way. God doesn't need anything to work with; he can create something out of nothing.

Look again at Romans 4:17: *"Abraham believed [in] God."* It wasn't just positive thinking that Abraham believed in. Positive thinking is fine (after all, what's the alternative?), but positive thinking is not faith. Positive thinking works in situations you have control over. But when you face things out of your control, you need more than a positive attitude. You need faith in God because only God can control what you can't control—and most of life is beyond your control. That's why you need faith far more than you need positive thinking.

In Luke 18:27, Jesus said, *"What is impossible with man is possible with God."*[7] God specializes in the impossible. That's why it's important to remember what God can do.

Rely on What God Has Said

Romans 4:18 says, *"Abraham, when hope was dead within him, went on hoping in faith. . . . He relied on the word of God."*[8] How do you know when hope is dead within you? You start using the word *never*: I'm *never* going to graduate. I'm *never* going to get well. I'm *never* going to get out of debt. I'm *never* going to forget all that shame and heartache. I'm *never* going to change. I'm *never* going to become what God wants me to be.

What should you do when your hope starts to fade? Scripture says to keep on hoping, just like

Abraham did. Look at Romans 4:18 again: *"Abraham, when hope was dead within him, went on hoping in faith. . . . He relied on the word of God."* When you are at a dead end, tap into your source of strength, the Bible. It's a treasure trove of hope. Read it. Study it. Memorize it. Meditate on it. The Word of God will revive your faith. It will renew your hope. It will strengthen your grip on God. Nothing else will encourage you like the Bible.

A dead end is a test of your faith. The Bible says, *"While God was testing him, Abraham still trusted in God and his promises, and so he offered up his son Isaac."*[9] When God said he wanted Abraham to sacrifice his son, Abraham didn't blink an eye. He didn't panic, because he remembered what God could do and he relied on what God had promised him. As they were walking up the hill to make the sacrifice, Abraham said to the servants, *"We will come back to you."*[10] When Isaac asked him, "Where's the sacrifice?" Abraham said, *"God himself will provide."*[11]

Abraham was at a dead end. But deliverance was coming.

When they reached the place God had told him about, Abraham built an altar there and arranged the wood on it. He bound his son Isaac and laid him on the altar, on top of the wood. Then he reached out his hand and took the knife to slay his son. But the angel of the LORD called out to him from heaven, "Abraham! Abraham!" . . .

Abraham looked up and there in a thicket he saw a ram caught by its horns. He went over and took the ram and sacrificed it as a burnt offering instead of his son.[12]

It wasn't until the knife was in the air that God provided a way out.

What happens when you reach a dead end and God asks you to give up the dream you thought he gave you? Can you do that in faith? Can you believe God will deliver you? Abraham did everything God told him to do. He passed the test of faith.

When you're at a dead end, remember what God can do, and rely on what God has said. Take him at his word.

Face the Facts with Faith

Romans 4:19–20 says, "*Without weakening in his faith, [Abraham] faced the fact that his body was as good as dead . . . and that Sarah's womb was also dead. Yet he did not waver through unbelief."*[13] Abraham was ninety-nine years old. Sarah was ninety years old and barren—and yet God said they would have a child. It was a medical impossibility. They were well beyond their childbearing years. But the Bible says Abraham faced the facts and yet he did not waver through unbelief.

Faith is not denying reality. It's not pretending you don't have a problem. Faith is not saying, "I'm not in pain" when you're miserable or, "I'm happy" when you're grieving inside. That's not faith; that's denial. Faith is facing the facts without being discouraged by them. Faith is believing that God is greater than your problems.

> **Faith is facing the facts without being discouraged by them.**

The key to faith is to look beyond your temporary circumstances and to focus on your eternal God. The Bible says, *"We fix our eyes not on what is seen, but on what is unseen, since what is seen* [the problem] *is temporary, but what is unseen* [God's power] *is eternal."*[14] It all has to do with focus.

When you face a dead end, remember what God can do, rely on what God has said, and face the facts with faith. Then, there is one more step.

Expect God to Deliver You

Abraham said to Isaac, *"God himself will provide the lamb for the burnt offering."*[15] Abraham expected God to deliver him. And because of his unwavering faith, Abraham was unwavering in his obedience. He did exactly what God told him to do.

This is an important lesson about faith. Faith isn't just saying you believe God; it's living like you believe God. As the Bible says, *"Faith by itself, if it is not accompanied by action, is dead. . . . I will show you my faith by my deeds."*[16]

What are you expecting God to do in your current situation? You may not be expecting him to do anything at all. But God works in your life according to your expectation. Jesus said, *"According to your faith let it be done to you."*[17] What are you believing God will do?

God works in your life according to your expectation.

The apostle Paul understood the principle of expectation: expectation gives birth to determination. Paul expected God to act. Therefore, Paul was determined to press through his dead end. He wrote, *"We were under great pressure, far beyond our ability to endure, so that we despaired of life itself. . . . But this happened that we might not rely on ourselves but on God, who raises the dead. He has delivered us . . . and he will deliver us . . . [and] we have set our hope that he will continue to deliver us."*[18]

Paul had reached the end of his rope. He wondered if the dream was over. But he knew God had delivered him in the past, so he trusted God to deliver him in the present and he believed God would deliver him in the future. Paul refused to give up hope.

If you have reached a dead end, do what Paul did. Remember what God has done, and believe he will do it again. Hold on to hope. Deliverance is coming.

CHAPTER 7

Expecting
Deliverance

The one who calls you is
faithful, and he will do it.
1 Thessalonians 5:24 (NIV)

Your dead end is the doorway to God's deliverance. In Moses's case, God made a way where there was no way. With their backs against the sea and Pharaoh's army bearing down on them, the Israelites faced a hopeless dead end. But their deliverance was coming.

God said to Moses, "*'Raise your staff and stretch out your hand over the sea to divide the water so that the Israelites can go through the sea on dry ground.'... Then Moses stretched out his hand over the sea, and all that night the* LORD *drove the sea back with a strong east wind and turned it into dry land. The waters were divided, and the Israelites went through the sea on dry ground, with a wall of water on their right and on their left.*"[1] When the Israelites had safely reached the other side, God caused the waters to flow back to their place, and the enemy army drowned in the sea.

God led his people to that dead end for a purpose. He wanted to teach them to trust him, and he wanted to display his glory.

What does God want to teach you in your dead end?

In the gospel of Matthew, we find the account of Jesus walking on the water. The Bible says, *"Immediately [Jesus] made the disciples get into the boat and go before him to the other side, while he dismissed the crowds. And after he had dismissed the crowds, he went up on the mountain by himself to pray. When evening came, he was there alone, but the boat by this time was a long way from the land, beaten by the waves, for the wind was against them. And in the fourth watch of the night he came to them, walking on the sea."*[2]

Don't miss the fact that the disciples were in the storm because they had obeyed Jesus. They were doing exactly what he told them to do. Now they were afraid they were going to die, and Jesus was nowhere to be found. In their minds, he was still back on shore where they had left him.

Notice the sequence of events: The disciples set sail during daylight, when the sun was out and the skies were clear. Then, when evening came, the storm arose and pummeled their boat all night long. The disciples knew they were powerless to control the situation. During the fourth watch of the night, Jesus came to them, walking on the water. The fourth watch of the night was from 3:00 a.m. to 6:00 a.m. In other words, Jesus didn't show up at the first sign of trouble. The miracle happened in the disciples' darkest hour.

What hour is it for you? How long have you been sailing in your storm? No matter how dark your situation is, your Deliverer is coming—and he just might show up in a way you've never seen before.

So, what is the key to deliverance? You have a choice: You can worry or worship, panic or praise. One way you can do that is by expressing gratitude in advance.

> No matter how dark your situation is, your Deliverer is coming—and he just might show up in a way you've never seen before.

The Key to Deliverance

The key to deliverance is faith-filled gratitude. When you're at a dead end and it seems like your dream will never come to pass, thank God that your deliverance is already on its way—even if you don't see it yet. Thanking God in advance is a big step of faith—and God always responds to faith! Jesus himself taught us to do this.

In John 11, we find the account of the resurrection of Lazarus. Jesus was in Jerusalem when his friends Mary and Martha sent word to him from the town of Bethany that their brother, Lazarus, was sick. They needed Jesus to heal him. Bethany was only about two miles away, but it took Jesus three days to get there. By the time Jesus arrived, Lazarus had died. He had already been in the grave four days. Jesus was too late, or so they thought. Mary and Martha both said, "Lord, if you had been here, our brother would not have died." But Jesus didn't come to heal Lazarus. He came to resurrect him.

Jesus didn't come to heal Lazarus. He came to resurrect him.

You may think you know the best answer to your dilemma. You may think you have it all figured out. You've been telling God exactly what he should do, how he should do it, and when he should do it. But God is God, and you're not! You need to let him do things his way and in his time. Always leave room for God to exceed your expectations.

Jesus told the people to roll the stone away from Lazarus's tomb. Then he looked up and said, *"Father, I thank you that you have heard me."*[3] Jesus thanked God in advance! This is the key to deliverance. After he had thanked God for answering his prayer, Jesus shouted, *"Lazarus, come forth."*[4] And Lazarus walked out of the grave.

Abraham also understood the principle of faith-filled gratitude. The Bible says, *"Abraham never doubted. . . . [He] praised God for this blessing even before it happened. He was completely sure that God was well able to do anything he promised."*[5] Notice it says Abraham praised God "even before it happened"—before the dream that God would make him into a great nation was fulfilled.

When you thank God for something after it happens, that's gratitude. But when you thank God for something before it happens, that is faith. That's what Jesus and Abraham did, and it is the highest form of faith—thanking God ahead of time for what you believe he will do. It's saying, "God, I don't know how you're going to make the dream you've given me come true. I'm at a dead end. But I thank you in advance that you

> When you thank God for something before it happens, that is faith.

know what you're doing and that you are going to work all things together for my good" (Romans 8:28).

Our Greatest Deliverance

Imagine the heartache and despair of the disciples when they saw Jesus hanging on the cross. Their friend, their teacher, the one in whom they had placed their hope, the one to whom they had dedicated their lives for the past three years was dead. They had thought Jesus was going to set up his kingdom and that they would be rulers with him. Now it was all over. How was it possible that the Messiah, the Son of God, was dead? They had come to the end of their dream. All hope was gone.

They didn't realize that God specializes in turning crucifixions into resurrections. For three days, Jesus's body lay lifeless in a tomb guarded by Roman soldiers. But on the third day, Jesus rose from the dead. It was the greatest deliverance in history.

Jesus's dead end proved to be the end of death. The sentence of death and eternal separation from God was overturned. Though we die physically, our souls can live eternally in the presence of God in heaven—our ultimate promised land.

Three Types of Deliverance

There are three primary ways God delivers you: external, internal, and eternal deliverance. When God delivers you externally, he miraculously alters your circumstances, as he did with the Israelites when he *"delivered [them] from the hand of the Egyptians."*[6] God intervenes, and the Red Sea parts. This will happen many times in your life, but it won't happen all the time.

Other times God delivers you not by changing the circumstances but by changing *you*. This is God's internal deliverance. He gives you a new dream, a new attitude, or a new perspective. God didn't change Paul's circumstances when he was in a dungeon in Rome, chained to a prison guard. But God did change his perspective. Paul wrote to his friends, *"I want you to know, my dear brothers and sisters, that everything that has happened to me here has helped to spread the Good News."*[7] Because Paul knew his pain had a greater purpose, he was better prepared to handle delays, difficulties, and dead ends.

God's third and ultimate form of deliverance is heaven. This is God's eternal deliverance—and it will be forever. God has not promised to remove all your pain in this world. God has not promised to solve every problem in the way you want it to be solved. God has not promised to keep all your loved ones alive for the rest of your life. There is pain in the world. There is sorrow and suffering. But remember, this is not heaven, this is earth. Your ultimate deliverance will come one day in heaven, where there will be no more pain or sorrow, no more sickness or suffering, no more heartache or disappointment.

No matter how God delivers you, his deliverance is guaranteed, *"for God can be trusted to keep his promise."*[8] He may not deliver you in the way you think he should, but he will deliver you in the way he knows is best. He has promised to complete the good work he has started in you (Philippians 1:6), and he will not make you wait one moment longer than he knows is necessary to accomplish his work in you.

What should be your first response when God delivers you? Celebrate! Rejoice! That's what Paul did. God delivered him after he'd been shipwrecked, beaten, and imprisoned. And even though Paul continued to face troubles, he still chose to say, *"Rejoice in the Lord always. I will say it again: Rejoice!"*[9]

It is your choice to rejoice.

Maybe you're at a dead end today and you don't

feel like rejoicing. You've been waiting on God for a miracle—a release from a hurt, an answer to a prayer, a breakthrough in an otherwise impossible situation—and you are losing hope that God's dream will come true.

Or maybe God has given you a specific promise that's not ending the way you believed it would or according to what you know to be true in Scripture. You've held on to it for a long time, and now you're tempted to let go.

You need to remember that God is not limited by your time on earth to fulfill his promises. Jesus said, *"Heaven and earth will pass away, but my words will never pass away."*[10] You can still hold on to the truth without insisting that the promise be fulfilled on your timetable. God has all of eternity to keep his Word!

So start thanking God right now for the deliverance that is already on its way. Jesus can take that hopeless end and turn it into an endless hope. Even if you face many dead ends, God will deliver you over and over again on earth, and then ultimately in heaven one day. Why? Because the *"steadfast love of the Lord never ceases; his mercies never come to an end; they are new every morning."*[11]

You see, God is a God of second chances. God is a God of newness. He doesn't do the same old things all the time. He'll often give you multiple dreams throughout your lifetime. The Bible says, *"In the last days, God says, I will pour out my Spirit on all people. Your sons and daughters will prophesy, your young men will see visions, your old men will dream dreams."*[12]

But to live out the dreams God has for your life, you need to embrace the new things God wants to do in your family, in your career, in your friendships, in his church, and in the world around you. And God wants you to *watch* for the new things he's going to do. He says in Isaiah 43:18–19, *"Do not cling to events of the past or dwell on what happened long ago. Watch for the new thing I am going to do. It is happening already—you can see it now!"*[13]

So trust him. Hold on to him. And remember, *"God can do anything, you know—far more than you could ever imagine or guess or request in your wildest dreams! He does it not by pushing us around but by working within us, his Spirit deeply and gently within us."*[14]

God's dream for your life has been on his mind since he formed you in your mother's womb. What he calls you to do, he will enable you to do—in his timing and in his way. You don't have any right to complain, gripe, argue, or doubt, because he's going to do it. He is faithful. But he will take you through these six phases of faith: from the dream to decision to delay to difficulties to a dead end and to deliverance. And he will take you through them many times; they're not a one-time experience. In

What he calls you to do, he will enable you to do.

Psalm 50:15, God says, "*I want you to trust me in your times of trouble, so I can rescue you and you can give me glory.*"[15]

Never give up on the dreams God created you to dream. He will never give up on you.

One Last Thing . . .

I'm so glad you're taking steps to discover and follow God's dream for your life.

I've often thought that extraordinary people are just ordinary people who attach themselves to an extraordinary dream—God's dream. And I'm convinced that nothing else in life will provide a greater sense of fulfillment than doing what God made you to do.

To encourage you as you move toward all God has for you, I created Daily Hope—my FREE email devotional and podcast that delivers Bible teaching to your inbox every day. Connecting to Daily Hope will inspire you to study God's Word and build a deep, meaningful relationship with him, which is essential to living the life you were meant to live.

I'm excited to help guide you on your journey, because pursuing God's dream is the greatest adventure you will ever experience.

Pastor Rick

Take the Next Step . . .
Get my FREE Daily Hope devotional at **PastorRick.com/Dream**

PASTOR RICK'S
DAILY HOPE

I Would Love to
Connect With You!

Get biblical hope and encouragement
delivered to your inbox every day with my
FREE Daily Hope devotional and podcast.

PastorRick.com/Dream

Reflection
Questions

Based on the principles taught throughout the book, the following questions will help you further understand the process God uses to fulfill the dream he gives you. Take time to reflect on them during your personal study time or small group discussion.

Chapter 1: How Faith and Dreaming Are Connected
- A great dream is a statement of faith.
  - Think of the biggest dream you have dreamed or could dream for your life. How does it reflect your faith in God?
- While you're working on your dream, God will be working on your character.

- In what ways do you want God to help you grow spiritually and emotionally while you are pursuing his dream for your life?
- Figuring out and following God's dream is a walk of faith.
    - Why do you think God doesn't give you your dream all at once and instead makes it a gradual, step-by-step process?
- Where God guides, he provides.
    - What do you need to ask God to provide for you today so that you can continue to pursue his dream for you?

Chapter 2: Discovering God's Dream for You

- Without a dream, you will always struggle with your identity—who you are.
    - What dream God has called you to follow? Have you ever considered your dream to be part of your identity? Why or why not?
- God's dream will never contradict God's Word.
    - How can you know if your dream contradicts what the Bible says?
- Both dreams and discouragement are contagious.
    - Think about the friends closest to you. In what ways are they encouraging you to pursue

God's dream? In what ways are they discouraging you?

- Nothing is more important than fulfilling God's dream for you. It's the reason he created you.
  - What are the things that compete most for your focus and keep you from committing to God's dream? What steps can you take to prioritize God's dream for your life?

Chapter 3: Deciding to Act

- The decision phase is not about making quick decisions. It's about making the *right* decisions.
  - What is one step you can take today to know God's Word better so you can make wise decisions?
- The problem is that we often would rather *appear* wise than *be* wise.
  - Who is the wisest person you know? In what ways do they model humility?
- Never confuse decision-making with problem-solving.
  - In what ways can you prepare yourself spiritually and emotionally for the problems you will encounter when pursuing your dream?

Chapter 4: Persisting through Delays

- They were delayed because they were afraid.
  - What is one way you can overcome your fear?
- There is always a delay between sowing and reaping.
  - What characteristics of Jesus Christ do you want God to grow in you while you wait on your dream to come to fruition? Pray, and ask him to develop and mature you in those ways so you will be faithful even in the delay.
- A delay is not a denial.
  - How do you respond to God when he says, "Not yet" to your request, instead of saying, "No"? How do you think he wants you to respond to both answers?

Chapter 5: Dealing with Difficulties

- With any opportunity, you need to ask if it is what God wants.
  - Why is it important to have trustworthy Christlike people around you when trying to decide if an opportunity is from God? Who are those people in your life?
- What happens *to* you is not nearly as important as what happens *in* you.

- What is the most difficult trial you have ever been through? How did it change you in ways that have eternal significance?
- Troubles don't come to stay; they come to pass.
  - When you need to remind yourself that your troubles are only temporary, what eternal truths can you dwell on instead?

Chapter 6: Facing Dead Ends

- When you face a dead end, don't focus on what you *can't* do; focus on what God *can* do.
  - Why do you think God wants you to come to a point where you understand that you cannot do everything in your own strength?
- Faith is facing the facts without being discouraged by them.
  - If you believe that God is greater than your problems, what will look different about the way you face difficult circumstances?
- God works in your life according to your expectation.
  - What is one way you can *show* God what you expect him to do in your dead end instead of just telling him?

Chapter 7: Expecting Deliverance

- No matter how dark your situation is, your Deliverer is coming—and he just might show up in a way you've never seen before.
  - How will you worship God today while you wait on him to provide deliverance from your difficulty?
- Jesus didn't come to heal Lazarus. He came to resurrect him.
  - As you pray for deliverance and ask God for specific requests, how can you leave room in your prayers for him to exceed your expectations?
- When you thank God for something before it happens, that is faith.
  - What do you believe God is going to do for you as your go after your dream? Thank him in advance for it right now and pray, "God, I don't know how you're going to make the dream you've given me come true. But I thank you in advance that you know what you're doing and that you are going to work all things together for my good."
- What he calls you to do, he will enable you to do.

- In what specific ways has God gifted and prepared you for the dream he's given you? Will you trust him to provide in all the ways you cannot see or understand right now?

Notes

Chapter 1: How Faith and Dreaming Are Connected

1. Genesis 1:27.
2. (NIV).
3. John 1:3-4 (NCV).
4. Hebrews 11:6 (NIV).
5. 1 Timothy 6:7 (NIV).
6. Philippians 1:6 (NLT).
7. Proverbs 14:12 (NCV).
8. Ephesians 2:10 (NIV).
9. (NIV).
10. (MSG).
11. Ephesians 3:20 (MSG).
12. Proverbs 4:18 (NLT).
13. (NIV).
14. Mark 9:23 (GNT).
15. Matthew 9:29 (NIV).
16. 2 Corinthians 1:8-9 (PHILLIPS).
17. Ephesians 3:20 (MSG).

Chapter 2: Discovering God's Dream for You

1. Hebrews 11:6 (NIV).
2. Romans 12:2 (NIV).
3. Jeremiah 29:11 (NIV).
4. (GNT).
5. Romans 12:2 (GNT).
6. (TLB).
7. (NLT).
8. John 1:12 (NIV).
9. (GNT).
10. 1 Peter 4:10 (TLB).
11. (NIV).
12. Proverbs 27:17 (NLT).
13. 1 Corinthians 15:33 (NIV).
14. 1 Thessalonians 5:24 (NIV).
15. Acts 20:24 (GNT).

Chapter 3: Deciding to Act

1. James 1:5 (CEV).
2. (TLB).
3. Proverbs 3:13 (NIV).
4. Colossians 3:15 (GNT).
5. Proverbs 13:16 (NIV).
6. Proverbs 18:13 (TLB).
7. (GNT).
8. (NIV).
9. Psalm 119:70 (NLT).
10. (GNT).

11. (NIV).
12. Luke 14:28, 31 (NLT).
13. John 16:33 (NIV).
14. Proverbs 22:3 (TLB).
15. (TLB).
16. Ecclesiastes 11:4 (TLB).
17. (NIV).

Chapter 4: Persisting through Delays

1. Exodus 13:17–18 (NLT).
2. Deuteronomy 8:2 (TLB).
3. (PHILLIPS).
4. Proverbs 29:25 (TLB).
5. (ESV).
6. Hebrews 13:5 (GNT).
7. Numbers 21:4–5 (GNT).
8. Psalm 37:7–8 (TLB).
9. (GNT).
10. Philippians 4:8–9 (TLB).
11. (TLB).
12. Numbers 14:2, 4 (NIV).
13. Galatians 6:9 (KJV).
14. Luke 18:1 (PHILLIPS).
15. Psalm 106:7–8 ([GNT], 13 [NABRE]).
16. (TLB).
17. 2 Peter 3:9 (NJB).
18. Habakkuk 2:3 (TLB).

Chapter 5: Dealing with Difficulties

1. (NIV).
2. 2 Corinthians 11:23–28 (MSG).
3. 2 Corinthians 4:16 (MSG).
4. (GNT).
5. (NIV).
6. (NIV).
7. (NIV).
8. Psalm 73:16–17 (GNT).
9. (TLB).
10. (NIV).
11. (NIV).
12. (NIV).
13. (NIV).
14. 2 Corinthians 4:16–17 (NIV).
15. John 8:32 (NIV).
16. Proverbs 28:13 (TLB).
17. (NIV).
18. Hebrews 13:5 (ESV).

Chapter 6: Facing Dead Ends

1. Exodus 12:31 (NLT).
2. Exodus 14:13–14 (NIV).
3. Isaiah 7:9 (NIV).
4. Genesis 22:2 (NIV).
5. Hebrews 11:19 (TLB).
6. Romans 4:17 (NCV).
7. (NIV).

8. (PHILLIPS).
9. Hebrews 11:17 (TLB).
10. Genesis 22:5 (NIV).
11. Genesis 22:8 (NIV).
12. Genesis 22:9–13 (NIV).
13. (NIV).
14. 2 Corinthians 4:18 (NIV).
15. Genesis 22:8 (NIV).
16. James 2:17–18 (NIV).
17. Matthew 9:29 (NIV).
18. 2 Corinthians 1:8–10 (NIV).

Chapter 7: Expecting Deliverance

1. Exodus 14:16, 21–22 (NIV).
2. Matthew 14:22–25 (ESV).
3. John 11:41 (NIV).
4. John 11:43 (KJV).
5. Romans 4:20–21 (TLB).
6. Exodus 14:30 (ISV).
7. Philippians 1:12 (NLT).
8. Hebrews 10:23 (NLT).
9. Philippians 4:4 (NIV).
10. Matthew 24:35 (NIV).
11. Lamentations 3:22–23 (ESV).
12. Acts 2:17 (NIV).
13. (GNT).
14. Ephesians 3:20 (MSG).
15. (TLB).